WOLVES

by Mari Schuh

Raintree is an imprint of Capstone Global Library Limited, a company incorporated in England and Wales having its registered office at 264 Banbury Road, Oxford, OX2 7DY – Registered company number: 6695582

www.raintree.co.uk
myorders@raintree.co.uk

Text © Capstone Global Library Limited 2021
The moral rights of the proprietor have been asserted.

All rights reserved. No part of this publication may be reproduced in any form or by any means (including photocopying or storing it in any medium by electronic means and whether or not transiently or incidentally to some other use of this publication) without the written permission of the copyright owner, except in accordance with the provisions of the Copyright, Designs and Patents Act 1988 or under the terms of a licence issued by the Copyright Licensing Agency, Barnard's Inn, 86 Fetter Lane, London, EC4A 1EN (www.cla.co.uk). Applications for the copyright owner's written permission should be addressed to the publisher.

Edited by Mandy Robbins
Designed by Dina Her
Original illustrations © Capstone Global Library Limited 2021
Picture research by Morgan Walters
Production by Tori Abraham
Originated by Capstone Global Library Ltd

978 1 4747 9494 7 (hardback)
978 1 4747 9623 1 (paperback)

British Library Cataloguing in Publication Data
A full catalogue record for this book is available from the British Library.

Acknowledgements
We would like to thank the following for permission to reproduce photographs: Newscom: TOM & THERISA STACK/NHPA/Photoshot, 24; Shutterstock: Allison Coffin, 5, Benjamin B, 18, Bildagentur Zoonar GmbH, 6, 13, critterbiz, 25, David Dirga, 1, Dennis W Donohue, 20, Holly Kuchera, 11, Jearu, 17, Jim Cumming, 10, 14, Josef Pittner, 15, kochanowski, 12, Lillian Tveit, 7, Martin Mecnarowski, 23, Michael Roeder, 21, mjurik, 19, bottom 26-27, Red Squirrel, 9, Vlada Cech, Cover.

Every effort has been made to contact copyright holders of material reproduced in this book. Any omissions will be rectified in subsequent printings if notice is given to the publisher.

All the internet addresses (URLs) given in this book were valid at the time of going to press. However, due to the dynamic nature of the internet, some addresses may have changed, or sites may have changed or ceased to exist since publication. While the author and publisher regret any inconvenience this may cause readers, no responsibility for any such changes can be accepted by either the author or the publisher.

Printed and bound in India

WEST NORTHAMPTONSHIRE COUNCIL	
60000483240	
Askews & Holts	
WR	

Contents

Amazing wolves 4

Where wolves live 8

Wolf bodies 12

Eating 16

What wolves do 20

Dangers to wolves 26

   Fast facts 29

   Glossary 30

   Find out more 31

   Index 32

Words in **bold** are in the glossary.

Amazing wolves

A lost wolf howls at night. It is looking for its **pack**. The sound moves through the forest. It reaches more than 8 kilometres (5 miles) away.

Its pack hears the call. They howl back. Now the wolf knows where to go. It howls again.

Wolves howl for many reasons. They do it to hunt. They do it to find a **mate**. They warn others of danger.

Wolves are wild. They are related to dogs. Wolves are **mammals**. They have fur. Females feed milk to their young. They are also **warm-blooded**. Their body temperature is always the same.

People don't agree on how many types of wolves there are. Some other animals are a lot like wolves.

A common wolf is the grey wolf. Most have thick, grey fur. It can also be brown, red, black or white.

Where wolves live

Grey wolves live in North America, Europe and Asia. They live in wild areas.

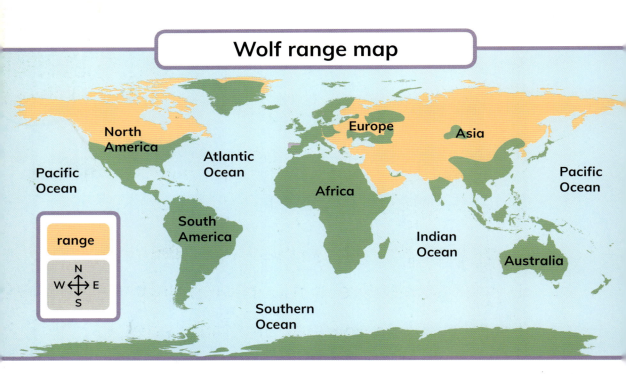

Wolves can live in almost every type of **habitat**. They can be found in grasslands. They also live in the **tundra**. They live in mountains and forests too. Wolves do not live in hot, damp rainforests. They do not live in very dry deserts.

Wolves live in groups called packs. Packs usually have six or seven wolves. They spend most of their time out in the open.

Female wolves give birth to pups in **dens**. Dens protect mothers and their young. Dens are usually **burrows** in the ground. Hollow logs can be dens too. Tree stumps and large cracks in rocks can also be dens. Dens keep young wolves safe.

Wolf bodies

Wolves have strong bodies. They can be different sizes. Some weigh about 45 kilograms (100 pounds). Others are smaller. They weigh only about 16 kg (35 pounds).

Wolves are natural hunters. They chase **prey**. Sharp teeth grab prey. They tear into meat. Wolves have big teeth and strong jaws for eating.

Wolves run fast! Long legs help them run far. Big feet help them to run for hours.

Thick fur keeps wolves warm and dry. Arctic wolves live in cold places. They have extra fur on their feet. They wrap their bushy tails around their bodies. A wolf's tail can cover its nose to keep it warm.

Fur helps keep wolves safe. The colour of their fur helps them to blend in. Wolves can be hard to see. Grey wolves blend in with land and trees. Arctic wolves are white. They blend in with the snow.

Eating

Wolves eat mostly meat. They can travel far to find animals to eat. They look for deer and moose. They also eat small animals such as rabbits. Sometimes wolves catch fish!

Wolves hunt mostly at night. A pack of wolves finds large animals to eat. They may look for old or sick animals. These animals are easier to catch. Wolves chase and attack them.

Wolves eat a lot. Most days they eat 1 to 2 kg (2 to 4 pounds) of food. Large wolves can eat 9 kg (20 pounds) of food at once! In the summer, packs may split up. Then wolves hunt alone.

Wolves can live for days without food. Sometimes they hide food for later and then dig it up when they need it.

What wolves do

Wolves live in packs. An adult male and female lead the pack. They are the **breeding** pair. They are in charge.

Each pack has its own **territory**. The pack roams the land. They guard their home area. They keep their group safe.

Wolves have many ways to send messages. They howl and growl. They bark and moan. A mother wolf moans when she is ready to feed her young. Wolves might stare to tell others to get away. A wolf might hold its tail up. This says that he is the leader.

Wolves have a very good sense of smell. They mark their home area with their poo and wee. Then other wolves stay away.

A wolf starts life as a small pup. A female gives birth to one **litter** each spring. She usually has four to six pups.

Pups drink their mother's milk for many weeks. Then wolves feed the pups chewed-up meat.

The pack takes care of the pups. Pups live with their pack for about two years. Then many leave. They look for a mate. Some start a family.

Dangers to wolves

For years, wolves were in danger. They could have died out. People were scared of them. Farmers didn't want wolves to hunt their animals. Many wolves were killed.

Today wolves face other dangers. People build roads where wolves live. It scares away some animals. Wolves there starve without enough food to eat.

Many people are working together to keep wolves from dying out. They are learning more about wolves. They are learning how they live and how to help them. Groups protect wolves and their homes. They work with farmers to protect both wolves and farm animals.

Wolves live in many areas today. The number of wolves is growing in many places.

Fast facts

Name: wolf

Habitat: grasslands, forests, tundra, mountains

Where in the world (range): North America, Europe, Asia

Food: elk, deer, moose, bison, bighorn sheep, caribou, musk oxen, beavers, squirrels, mice, birds, fish, lizards, snakes, fruit and vegetables

Predators: people

Life span: four to eight years in the wild

Glossary

breed mate and produce young

burrow hole in the ground made or used by an animal

den place where a wild animal may live

habitat where a plant or animal lives

litter group of animals born at the same time to the same mother

mammal warm–blooded animal that breathes air, has hair or fur, and feeds its young milk

mate join together to produce young

pack group of animals that hunts together

prey animal hunted by another animal

territory land on which an animal grazes or hunts for food and raises its young

tundra cold area where trees do not grow; the soil under the ground there is always frozen

warm-blooded having a body temperature that stays about the same all the time

Find out more

Books

Animals (DK findout!), DK (DK Children, 2016)

A Pack of Wolves: and Other Canine Groups (Animals in Groups), Anna Claybourne (Raintree, 2012)

Wolf: Killer King of the Forest (Top of the Food Chain), Angela Royston (Raintree, 2020)

Websites

www.bbc.co.uk/bitesize/topics/z6882hv/articles/zp92xnb
Learn more about mammals.

www.dkfindout.com/uk/animals-and-nature/dogs/wolves
Find out more about wolves.

Index

bodies 6, 12–13, 14
breeding pair 20

dangers 4, 26–27
dens 11

eating 13, 16, 18, 19, 22, 24, 27

fur 6, 7, 14, 15

hunting 4, 13, 16, 18, 26

jaws 13

mating 4, 25

packs 4, 10, 16, 18, 20, 21, 25
prey 13, 16
pups 6, 11, 22, 24–25

range 8–9
running 13

sizes 12
smelling 22
sounds 4, 22

tails 14, 22
teeth 13